How Ecosystems Change

by Ellen Chapman

PEARSON

Scott Foresman

DK

Ecosystems Change
Animals Change Ecosystems

In the 1860s, an amateur scientist near Boston accidentally introduced the gypsy moth caterpillar, an insect native to Europe, into the ecosystem. More than one hundred years later, this forest pest has spread throughout much of the eastern United States. It feeds on forest foliage, especially oak and aspen trees. In some areas, and in years when the caterpillars are most active, up to $\frac{1}{5}$ percent of trees in a particular forest may die.

The gypsy moth caterpillar can harm the environment. However, some animals change ecosystems in a helpful way. When animals such as earthworms burrow through the ground, they make holes that let more moisture into the soil. This helps plant roots to grow.

Gypsy moth caterpillar activity causes damage to trees.

People Change Ecosystems

Your backyard is an ecosystem. Think of how many ways it changes. Sometimes it is noticeable, and sometimes it is not. If you plant a vegetable garden, you are changing the ecosystem. You are providing food for yourself, but also taking away open space and nutrients from other animals.

When you cut down a tree, organisms that relied on it for everything from food to shade must turn elsewhere. They will have to adapt to the changed ecosystem. Their new ways of living will change how other organisms live in the ecosystem as well.

Ecosystems can be changed by people on a much larger scale as well. What if a forest fire wiped out a forest? What happens when **pesticides** kill all the insects in an ecosystem? In Maryland in 2002, it was discovered that the snakehead fish, a meat-eater native to Asia, had been introduced to a local pond. This new fish, nicknamed the "walking fish" because it has the ability to survive out of water and walk from pond to pond, has completely changed the pond's ecosystem.

Species Change

All organisms pass on traits to their young. These traits may change over time to help a species survive.

Inheriting DNA

Heredity is the process by which plants and animals **inherit** half of their genes from each parent. The genes control the way the organisms grow. But each offspring of the same parents is different because each one receives a unique mix of genes. This is one way offspring can change from generation to generation.

Children usually look a bit like each of their parents. But sometimes offspring show traits that neither of their parents have.

A child might be born with red hair, when both parents have brown hair. Nevertheless, this is still an inherited trait, because children get all of their genes from their parents.

DNA has the structure of a double helix.

What is not inherited?

Genes can determine much of what an organism is like. But the ecosystem also plays a role in how the organism grows. The color of organisms can be affected by their ecosystems. For example, plants need light to develop chlorophyll, which makes leaves green. Without enough light, some leaves can be a lighter shade of green.

Pale leaves have little chlorophyll.

This sprouting potato has been kept in the dark. The leaves and stems have little chlorophyll and are pale green.

Bright-green leaves are rich in chlorophyll.

After exposure to the sunlight, the potato plant's leaves and stems become rich in chlorophyll and turn bright green.

Adaptations

When ecosystems change, organisms that are best adapted to the change will fit into the ecosystem the best. One way that this can happen is for a **mutation,** or random change, to take place in an organism's genes. Often the mutation is harmful to the organism or has no effect. But sometimes the change helps the organism survive, so the change can be passed on to its offspring. The organisms that are best adapted to compete for food and shelter in a changed ecosystem survive very well. For example, if an ecosystem suddenly becomes colder, members of a species that are best adapted to the new temperature will survive.

webbed feet

flippers

The penguin is a bird that does not fly. Its wings have become flippers, and its feet are webbed. Both of these adaptations have enabled it to be at home in the sea.

Structural Adaptations

Some of these adaptations are called **structural adaptations.** This means a change in a body part of an organism that helps it survive in its ecosystem. For example, it is thought that giraffes with long necks were better at getting food from the tops of trees in the African savannah. The giraffe's ancestors had shorter necks. Then one was born with a slightly longer neck, allowing it to reach food that the other animals could not. This advantage was passed on through genes to new generations of giraffes. Over many years, many slight changes like this gave the giraffe the very long neck it has today. This process is called natural selection. Helpful adaptations are passed on, or selected, by nature.

Behavioral Adaptations

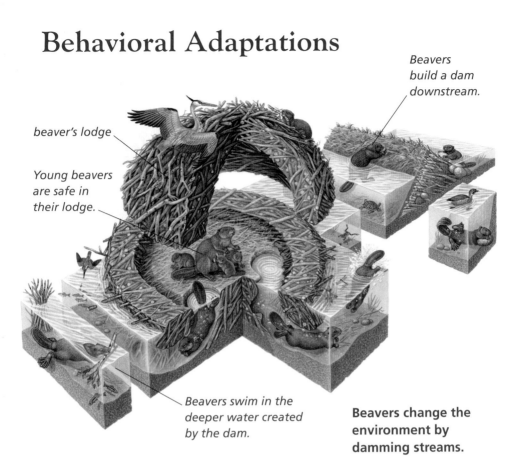

Beavers build a dam downstream.

beaver's lodge

Young beavers are safe in their lodge.

Beavers swim in the deeper water created by the dam.

Beavers change the environment by damming streams.

Another way organisms are adapted to changed ecosystems is by **behavioral adaptations.** These are changes in the way an organism acts that help it to survive. They are sometimes called instincts. For example, beavers are born knowing how to build dams. They inherit this instinct from their parents. The instinct to build a dam is a helpful adaptation that was caused by natural selection. Some behaviors are learned, not inherited. For example, chimpanzees sometimes use leaves to get water out of hollow trees. They crumple the leaves up and use them like sponges. This behavior is learned, and parents teach it to their offspring.

Changes Causing More Changes

When an organism changes, it can affect other organisms. This can cause the other organisms to change as well.

Behavior Changes

The way animals act can change for many reasons. Their actions might change if there has been a change in the number or types of animals in their ecosystem. For example, if one animal that is prey for a predator moves out of an ecosystem, the predator must find a new source of food. It may begin hunting a different animal. This new behavior might change the ecosystem a lot.

Population Changes

Organisms that are introduced into an ecosystem bring many changes. The alewife is a fish that originally bred in rivers, but made its home in the Atlantic Ocean. It is believed that in the 1800s, the alewife followed the Erie Canal when it left the ocean for a short time to breed. It eventually made its way to the Great Lakes. The fish never returned to salt water and became a major species of lake fish in its new home. In fact, the ecosystem of some of the Great Lakes is now very dependent on the alewife because it eats zooplankton, keeping the lakes clean. It also serves as food for larger organisms, such as salmon. Scientists know that removing the alewife from its adopted ecosystem would cause lots of problems. Instead, they are focusing on keeping the alewife population stable.

When the Erie Canal was built in 1825, it allowed the alewife to enter the Great Lakes.

You may have heard of "strep throat" and may have even had it. The illness is caused by the streptococcus bacteria. The bacteria produce toxins, which can harm the body. In most cases, medicines called antibiotics can kill streptococcus. But one type of the bacteria has adapted and now survives some antibiotics. This makes it very hard to cure, and dangerous to people.

Today many bacteria are adapting to survive antibiotics. Scientists are always looking for new medicines to use when bacteria adapt to the old ones.

streptococcus bacteria

What is extinction?

If a plant or animal is not adapted to changes in its ecosystem, it will try to move, or migrate, to another place. But if the organism cannot move, or there is nowhere left to go, the size of its population will shrink, and the species may become **extinct.** That means that there are no members of its kind alive. Many species are becoming extinct as people move into other organisms' habitats, taking away their homes and food supplies.

Dinosaurs are probably the best-known extinct animals.

One recent example of extinction in the United States is the dusky seaside sparrow, which became extinct in 1987. It had lived on the east coast of Florida, but its habitat was reduced as highways and building development spread to more areas. From now on, scientists will only know about the dusky seaside sparrow from reading records kept about it.

Animals that became extinct a very long time ago can be studied by their fossils. Fossils are remains of plants and animals that are no longer living. There are many different reasons why species become extinct. Fossils give scientists information about what past ecosystems and species were like and what caused their extinction.

Fossils have also shown scientists that many species have become extinct in the past. In any ecosystem, some organisms will survive, and some will not.

The dusky seaside sparrow became extinct in 1987.

Other organisms that are close to being extinct are called endangered species. Organisms that are in less danger are called threatened species. The blue whale, the largest mammal that has ever lived, is an endangered species. For years it seemed as if this giant would become extinct. Beginning in the late 1800s, it was hunted for the oil its body contained. There may have been up to 350,000 blue whales in the world's oceans at that time. By 1931, they were highly endangered. Almost all of them had been killed. In 1966, the International Whaling Commission banned the hunting of blue whales. Today it is estimated that there are about ten thousand blue whales.

Ecosystems are always changing. Sometimes the change is natural. But often the change is caused by humans. These changes can be dangerous, causing whole species to disappear from the Earth forever. People must be careful in the way they treat the world and remember that it is shared with many other living things.

The blue whale is an endangered species.

Glossary

behavioral adaptation   a change in the way members of a species act that helps them to survive

extinct   when every member of a species has died and there are no members of that species left alive anywhere on Earth

inherit   to receive genes from one's parents

mutation   a random change in an organisms genes

pesticide   a poison that kills insects

structural adaptation   a change in a body part of an organism that helps it to survive